W9-BNT-691

Take a trip down memory lane with this look back at 1962. There is the Cuban Missile Crisis; astronaut John Glenn, onboard *Friendship 7*, is the first American to orbit Earth; Marilyn Monroe dies at the age of 36; and the Space Needle, built for this year's World's Fair held in Seattle, Washington, opens to the public. Remember the stories, photos, news, people, advertisements, sports and events that made 1962 your special year!

A walk back in time...

To:

From:

Managing Editor • Art Worthington

Publishers • Lawrence Siegel & Art Worthington

Cover Design • Peter Hess

Designer • Liz Howard

Writing & Research • Laurie Cohn

Facilitator • Pamela Thomas

FLICKBACK

.com

(800) 541-3533

at the MOVIES

A Very Private Affair • Advise And Consent • All Fall Down • Barabbas • Billy Budd • Birdman Of Alcatraz • Boccaccio '70 • Bon Voyage! • Boys' Night Out • The Brain That Wouldn't Die • The Cabinet Of Dr. Caligari • Cape Fear • The Chapman Report • The Children's Hour • Creation Of The Humanoids • David And Lisa • Days Of Wine And Roses • Divorce Italian Style • Dr. No • Experiment In Terror • Five Finger Exercise • The Four Horsemen Of The Apocalypse • Freud • Geronimo • Gigot • Gypsy • The Happy Thieves • Hatari! • How The West Was Won • The Interns • Jumbo • Kid Galahad • Lawrence Of Arabia • The Legend Of Lobo • Light In The Piazza • Lolita • The Loneliness Of The Long Distance Runner • Lonely Are The Brave • The Longest Day • Lover Come Back • The Man Who Shot Liberty Valance • The Manchurian Candidate • The Miracle Worker • Mr. Hobbs Takes A Vacation • The Music Man • Mutiny On The Bounty • My Geisha • No Exit • The Notorious Landlady • Nude On The Moon • Only Two Can Play • Panic In Year Zero! • Period Of Adjustment • The Phantom Of The Opera • Requiem For A Heavyweight • The Road To Hong Kong • Rome Adventure • Satan Never Sleeps • Sergeants 3 • The Slime People • Smog • The Spiral Road • Strangers In The City • Sweet Bird Of Youth • Tender Is The Night • That Touch Of Mink • This Is Not A Test • To Kill A Mockingbird • Two For The Seesaw • Two Weeks In Another Town • The Underwater City • The Valiant • Walk On The Wild Side • Waltz Of The Toreadors • What Ever Happened To Baby Jane? • The Weird Ones • Yojimbo

Oscars® Presented in 1962

BEST PICTURE
WEST SIDE STORY

BEST ACTOR
MAXIMILIAN SCHELL, *Judgment At Nuremberg*

BEST ACTRESS
SOPHIA LOREN, *Two Women*

BEST DIRECTOR
ROBERT WISE, JEROME ROBBINS
West Side Story

BEST SUPPORTING ACTOR
GEORGE CHAKIRIS, *West Side Story*

BEST SUPPORTING ACTRESS
RITA MORENO, *West Side Story*

BEST SONG
"MOON RIVER," *Breakfast At Tiffany's*

LOREN

1962 Favorites
(Oscars® Presented in 1963)

BEST PICTURE
LAWRENCE OF ARABIA

BEST ACTOR
GREGORY PECK, *To Kill A Mockingbird*

BEST ACTRESS
ANNE BANCROFT, *The Miracle Worker*

BEST DIRECTOR
DAVID LEAN, *Lawrence Of Arabia*

BEST SUPPORTING ACTOR
ED BEGLEY, *Sweet Bird Of Youth*

BEST SUPPORTING ACTRESS
PATTY DUKE, *The Miracle Worker*

BEST SONG
"DAYS OF WINE AND ROSES,"
Days Of Wine And Roses

PECK

Tippi Hedren, Alfred Hitchcock's new discovery, stars in his upcoming film, *The Birds*, about which Hitchcock comments that his 700 trained bird actors work for birdseed.

Hedren

Sophia Loren sues Bronston Productions for putting her name below **Charlton Heston**'s on a Broadway billboard advertising *El Cid*.

Dean Martin bows out of *Something's Got To Give* after his leading lady **Marilyn Monroe** is dropped from the movie. Monroe is fired by 20th Century Fox and is sued for damages after she misses 20 out of 32 workdays. Gossip columnist **Hedda Hopper** predicts that Marilyn is at the end of her road.

Monroe

Loren

NEW
MOVIE
STARS

Ann-Margret
  Richard Beymer
Bobby Darin
    Tippi Hedren
Peter Falk
  Yvette Mimieux
George Peppard
Suzanne Pleshette

Pleshette

Peppard

This is NEW!

WE USEFUL PROTEINS PROUDLY PRESENT THE HAPPIEST TASTING PROTEIN CEREAL EVER CREATED...

This is Life

WE'RE NO ORDINARY PROTEIN! WE'RE 100% AS USEFUL AS THE PROTEIN IN MEAT!

100% AS USEFUL AS THE PROTEIN IN MILK!

Life has The Most Useful Protein

—EVER IN A READY-TO-EAT CEREAL!

WHAT A DIFFERENCE IN PROTEIN...

Some proteins are "lazy." They can't build your body. They lack the right amount of certain protein elements.

Some proteins are "hard working." They build, repair and maintain the body. You need working, useful proteins every day.

Life gives you "working" protein—the useful kind. Life's protein is 100% as useful as the protein in meat and milk!

Now from oats...nature's richest protein grain... Quaker brings you Life

Kids love the delicate sweetness that the sugar crystals inside Life add to its great toasty, oats taste.

Mothers love the protein build-up Life gives (and the way kids eat it up).

Everybody loves Life's special protein—useful protein—the same quality of protein you get in meat and milk!

YOU'LL LOVE LIFE

Life

MOST USEFUL PROTEIN
—ever in a ready-to-eat cereal

WHAT'S on TV?

The Adventures Of Ozzie & Harriet

The Andy Griffith Show

The Andy Williams Show

Bachelor Father

Beany And Cecil

Ben Casey

The Bob Newhart Show

Bonanza

The Bugs Bunny Show

The Bullwinkle Show

Candid Camera

Car 54, Where Are You?

Cheyenne

The Danny Thomas Show

Death Valley Days

The Defenders

Dennis The Menace

The Detectives

The Dick Powell Show

The Dick Van Dyke Show

The Dinah Shore Chevy Show

The Donna Reed Show

Dr. Kildare

The Ed Sullivan Show

Ensign O'Toole

Father Knows Best

Father Of The Bride

The Flintstones

The Garry Moore Show

Gunsmoke

Have Gun Will Travel

Hawaiian Eye

Hazel

It's A Man's World

I've Got A Secret

The Jack Benny Show

The Joey Bishop Show

Laramie

Lassie

The Lawrence Welk Show

Leave It To Beaver

The Many Loves Of Dobie Gillis

The Match Game

Maverick

Meet The Press

The Merv Griffin Show

Mister Ed

My Three Sons

Password

The Perry Como Show

Perry Mason

The Price Is Right

Rawhide

The Real McCoys

The Red Skelton Show

The Rifleman

Route 66

77 Sunset Strip

Tell It To Groucho

To Tell The Truth

The Twilight Zone

The Untouchables

What's My Line?

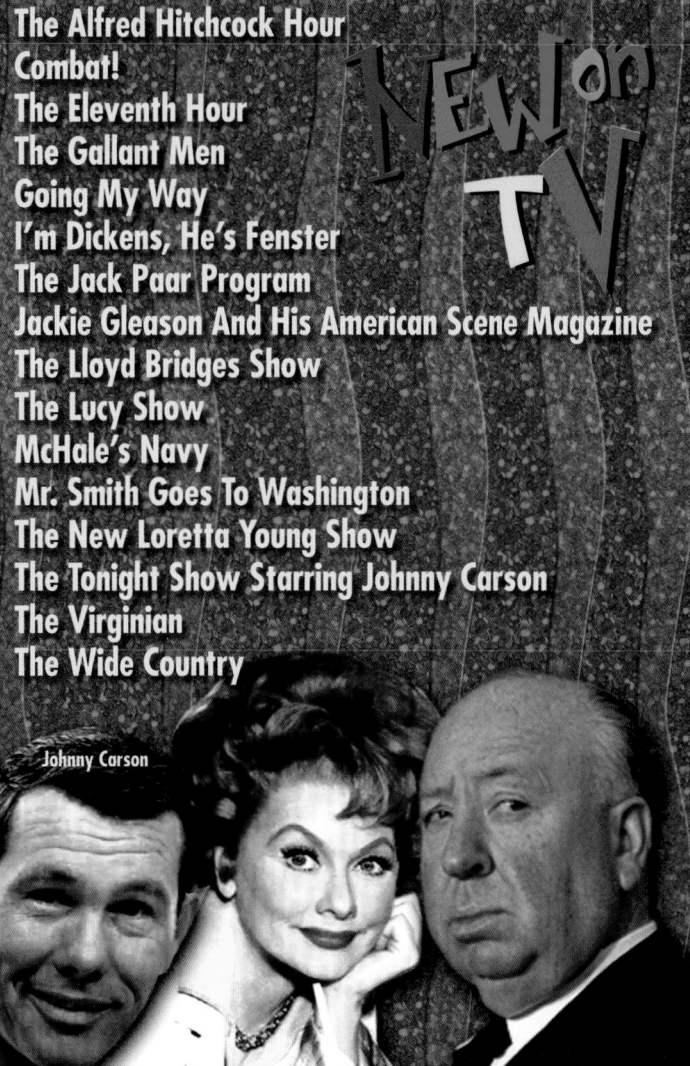

The Alfred Hitchcock Hour
Combat!
The Eleventh Hour
The Gallant Men
Going My Way
I'm Dickens, He's Fenster
The Jack Paar Program
Jackie Gleason And His American Scene Magazine
The Lloyd Bridges Show
The Lucy Show
McHale's Navy
Mr. Smith Goes To Washington
The New Loretta Young Show
The Tonight Show Starring Johnny Carson
The Virginian
The Wide Country

New on TV

Johnny Carson

Lucille Ball

Alfred Hitchcock

1962 Advertisement

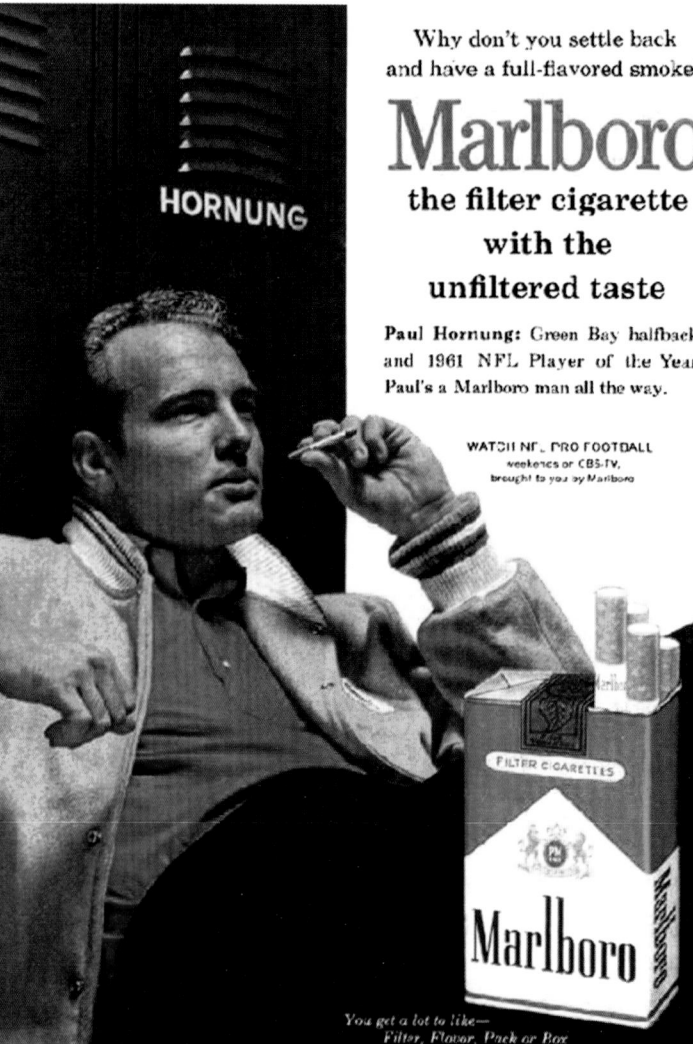

TOP TEN

October 1961 - April 1962

1. Wagon Train
2. Bonanza
3. Gunsmoke
4. Hazel
5. Perry Mason
6. The Red Skelton Show
7. The Andy Griffith Show
8. The Danny Thomas Show
9. Dr. Kildare
10. Candid Camera

October 1962 - April 1963

1. The Beverly Hillbillies
2. Candid Camera
3. The Red Skelton Show
4. Bonanza
5. The Lucy Show
6. The Andy Griffith Show
7. Ben Casey
8. The Danny Thomas Show
9. The Dick Van Dyke Show
10. Gunsmoke

1962 Advertisement

In one of the fastest climbs in television history, *The Beverly Hillbillies* takes the top spot in the Nielsen rat ings after only five weeks.

The Jetsons, the first pro gram to be carried by ABC in color, premieres.

With a penchant for pie-in-the-face humor, Detroit local **Soupy Sales** is picked up by ABC for a prime time spot.

Julia Child kicks off her PBS cooking show, *The French Chef*.

The Statue of Liberty, President Kennedy's news conference, a portion of a baseball game, pictures of buffalo and Indian chief in South Dakota are the first images transmitted to Europe using the new Telstar system. Europe responds and sends America shots of Big Ben in London, the Sistine Chapel and fishermen in Italy and reindeer in Sweden.

Series

Humor
The Bob Newhart Show

Drama
The Defenders

Variety
The Garry Moore Show

News
Huntley-Brinkley Report

Entertainers

Best Actor
E.G. Marshall,
The Defenders

Best Actress
Shirley Booth, *Hazel*

**Performer
(Variety Or Musical)**
Carol Burnett,
The Garry Moore Show

Comedy Writer
Carl Reiner,
The Dick Van Dyke Show

RADIO

In a speech before the National Association of Broadcasters, Newton Minow voices his concern over the uncertain economic health of the radio industry as one-third of the nation's radio stations report a loss.

183,800,000 radio sets are currently being used in American homes.

New York's WOR celebrates its 40th year on the air, with its successful 24-hour-a-day programming including over 20 hours of talk.

On the radio since 1942, the very popular program *Suspense* stops airing as does *Yours Truly, Johnny Dollar*, which began broadcasting in 1949.

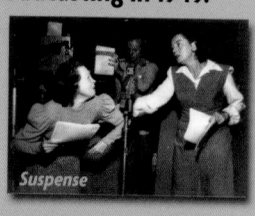

Suspense

With the help of Edward R. Murrow, CBS radio personality John Henry Faulk is awarded $2.8 million in a libel suit against a sponsor who accused him of being a Communist.

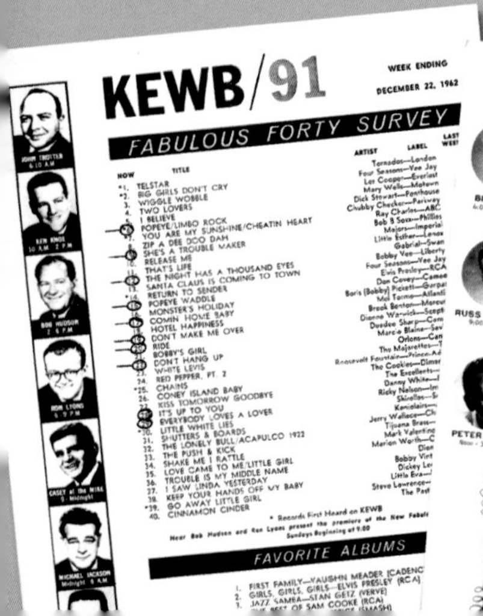

KEWB/91

WEEK ENDING DECEMBER 22, 1962

FABULOUS FORTY SURVEY

JOHN TROTTER 6-10 A.M
KEN KNOX 10 A.M. 2 P.M
BOB HUDSON 2 6 P.M.
RON LYONS 6-9 P.M
CASEY at the MIKE 9 - Midnight
MICHAEL JACKSON Midnight 6 A.M.

NOW TITLE

*1. TELSTAR
*2. BIG GIRLS DON'T CRY
3. WIGGLE WOBBLE
4. TWO LOVERS
5. I BELIEVE
6. POPEYE/LIMBO ROCK
*7. YOU ARE MY SUNSHINE/CHEATIN HEART
8. ZIP A DEE DOO DAH
9. SHE'S A TROUBLE MAKER
10. RELEASE ME
11. THAT'S LIFE
12. THE NIGHT HAS A THOUSAND EYES
13. SANTA CLAUS IS COMING TO TOWN
*14. RETURN TO SENDER
15. POPEYE WADDLE
16. MONSTER'S HOLIDAY
17. COMIN HOME BABY
18. HOTEL HAPPINESS
19. DON'T MAKE ME OVER
20. RIDE
21. BOBBY'S GIRL
22. DON'T HANG UP
23. WHITE LEVIS
24. RED PEPPER, PT. 2
*25. CHAINS
26. CONEY ISLAND BABY
27. KISS TOMORROW GOODBYE
28. IT'S UP TO YOU
29. EVERYBODY LOVES A LOVER
*30. LITTLE WHITE LIES
31. SHUTTERS & BOARDS
32. THE LONELY BULL/ACAPULCO 1922
33. THE PUSH & KICK
34. SHAKE ME I RATTLE
35. LOVE CAME TO ME/LITTLE GIRL
36. TROUBLE IS MY MIDDLE NAME
37. I SAW LINDA YESTERDAY
38. KEEP YOUR HANDS OFF MY BABY
*39. GO AWAY LITTLE GIRL
40. CINNAMON CINDER

ARTIST LABEL LAST WEEK

Tornados—London
Four Seasons—Vee Jay
Les Cooper—Everlast
Mary Wells—Motown
Dick Stewart—Penthouse
Chubby Checker—Parkway
Ray Charles—ABC
Bob B Soxx—Philles
Majors—Imperial
Little Esther—Lenox
Gabriel—Swan
Bobby Vee—Liberty
Four Seasons—Vee Jay
Elvis Presley—RCA
Dan Covey—Cameo
Boris (Bobby) Pickett—Garpax
Mel Torme—Atlanti
Brook Benton—Mercur
Dionne Warwick—Scept
Deedee Sharp—Cam
Marcie Blaine—Sev
Orlons—Can
The Majorettes—T
Roosevelt Fountain—Prince-Ad
The Cookies—Dimer
The Excellents—
Danny White—
Ricky Nelson—Im
Shirelles—S
Kenjolairs—
Jerry Wallace—Ch
Tijuana Brass—
Mark Valentino
Marion Worth—C
Dion
Bobby Vint
Dickey Le
Little Eva—
Steve Lawrence—
The Past

• Records First Heard on KEWB

Hear Bob Hudson and Ron Lyons present the premiere of the New Fabulo
Sundays Beginning at 9:00

FAVORITE ALBUMS

1. FIRST FAMILY—VAUGHN MEADER (CADENC
2. GIRLS, GIRLS, GIRLS—ELVIS PRESLEY (RCA)
3. JAZZ SAMBA—STAN GETZ (VERVE)

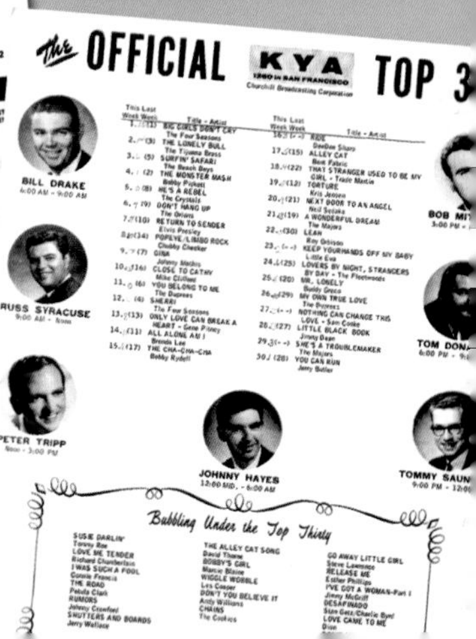

The OFFICIAL KYA TOP 3

KYA 1260 IN SAN FRANCISCO
Churchill Broadcasting Corporation

BILL DRAKE 6:00 AM - 9:00 AM
RUSS SYRACUSE 9:00 AM - Noon
PETER TRIPP Noon - 3:00 PM
JOHNNY HAYES 12:00 MID. - 6:00 AM
BOB MI 3:00 PM -
TOM DON 6:00 PM - 9:
TOMMY SAUN 9:00 PM - 12:0

This Week / Last Week / Title - Artist

1. (11) BIG GIRLS DON'T CRY - The Four Seasons
2. (3) THE LONELY BULL - The Tijuana Brass
3. (5) SURFIN' SAFARI - The Beach Boys
4. (2) THE MONSTER MASH - Bobby Pickett
5. (8) HE'S A REBEL - The Crystals
6. (9) DON'T HANG UP - The Orlons
7. (10) RETURN TO SENDER - Elvis Presley
8. (34) POPEYE/LIMBO ROCK - Chubby Checker
9. (7) GINA - Johnny Mathis
10. (16) CLOSE TO CATHY - Mike Clifford
11. (6) YOU BELONG TO ME - The Duprees
12. (4) SHERRI - The Four Seasons
13. (13) ONLY LOVE CAN BREAK A HEART - Gene Pitney
14. (11) ALL ALONE AM I - Brenda Lee
15. (17) THE CHA-CHA-CHA - Bobby Rydell
16. (- -) RIDE - DeeDee Sharp
17. (15) ALLEY CAT - Bent Fabric
18. (22) THAT STRANGER USED TO BE MY GIRL - Trade Martin
19. (12) TORTURE - Kris Jensen
20. (21) NEXT DOOR TO AN ANGEL - Neil Sedaka
21. (19) A WONDERFUL DREAM - The Majors
22. (30) LEAH - Roy Orbison
23. (- -) KEEP YOURHANDS OFF MY BABY - Little Eva
24. (25) LOVERS BY NIGHT, STRANGERS BY DAY - The Fleetwoods
25. (20) MR. LONELY - Buddy Greco
26. (29) MY OWN TRUE LOVE - The Duprees
27. (- -) NOTHING CAN CHANGE THIS LOVE - Sam Cooke
28. (27) LITTLE BLACK BOOK - Jimmy Dean
29. (- -) SHE'S A TROUBLEMAKER - The Majors
30. (28) YOU CAN RUN - Jerry Butler

Bubbling Under the Top Thirty

SUSIE DARLIN' - Tommy Roe
LOVE ME TENDER - Richard Chamberlain
I WAS SUCH A FOOL - Connie Francis
THE ROAD - Petula Clark
RUMORS - Johnny Crawford
SHUTTERS AND BOARDS - Jerry Wallace
THE ALLEY CAT SONG - David Thorne
BOBBY'S GIRL - Marcie Blaine
WIGGLE WOBBLE - Les Cooper
DON'T YOU BELIEVE IT - Andy Williams
CHAINS - The Cookies
GO AWAY LITTLE GIRL - Steve Lawrence
RELEASE ME - Esther Phillips
I'VE GOT A WOMAN-Part I - Jimmy McGriff
DESAFINADO - Stan Getz/Charlie Byrd
LOVE CAME TO ME - Dion

CHRYSLER '62 / features the new full-size 300
-a high performance sports series in a popular price range!

The new Chrysler 300's pedigree runs seven champions deep! From the best of the 300's built in '55 to last year's proud G! Chrysler's new full-size sports series is built for men who take their excitement straight! Three fired-up models! With prices that start only a few hundred dollars more than Newport, the full-size price surprise.

Remarkable automobiles! With such a wide selection of options you can almost design your own 300! Like deep leather contour seats! Power steering! A V-8 engine with the kick of 380 horses! You can choose any of these with your 300! Standard equipment includes torsion-bar suspension, still-rated best for smooth ride and handling by the experts . . . all-welded, rattle-repellent Unibody . . . battery-saving alternator and the biggest brakes in its class. Treat yourself to all the free thrills of a 300 sports ride. At your Chrysler dealer's today!

PLUS... A NEW FULL-
SIZE NEWPORT... still **$2,964.***

*CHRYSLER SUGGESTED RETAIL PRICE FOR 4-DOOR SEDAN. EXCLUSIVE OF DESTINATION CHARGES. WHITEWALL TIRES EXTRA.

NEWPORT ■ 300 ■ NEW YORKER . . . AGAIN NO JR. EDITIONS TO COMPROMISE YOUR INVESTMENT!

Baby, It's You *The Shirelles;* **Big Girls Don't Cry** *Frankie Valli & The 4 Seasons;* **Blowin' In The Wind** *Bob Dylan;* **Break It To Me Gently** *Brenda Lee;* **Breaking Up Is Hard To Do** *Neil Sedaka;* **Can't Help Falling In Love** *Elvis Presley;* **Cotton Fields** *The Highwaymen;* **Crying In The Rain** *The Everly Brothers;* **Devil Woman** *Marty Robbins;* **Do You Love Me** *The Contours;* **Don't Break The Heart That Loves You** *Connie Francis;* **Don't Hang Up** *The Orlons;* **Dream Baby** *Roy Orbison;* **Duke Of Earl** *Gene Chandler;* **Go Away Little Girl** *Steve Lawrence;* **Good Luck Charm** *Elvis Presley;* **Havin' A Party** *Sam Cooke;* **He's A Rebel** *The Crystals;* **I Can't Stop Loving You** *Ray Charles;* **It Keeps Right On A-Hurtin'** *Johnny Tillotson;* **I've Been Everywhere** *Hank Snow;* **Johnny Angel** *Shelley Fabares;* **Johnny Get Angry** *Joanie Sommers;* **Let Me In** *The Sensations;* **Letter Full Of Tears** *Gladys Knight & The Pips;* **Limbo Rock** *Chubby Checker;* **The Loco-Motion** *Little Eva;* **Love Letters** *Ketty Lester;* **The Man Who Shot Liberty Valance** *Gene Pitney;* **Mashed Potato Time** *Dee Dee Sharp;* **Misery Loves Company** *Porter Wagoner;* **Monster Mash** *Bobby "Boris" Pickett & The Crypt Kickers;* **The One Who Really Loves You** *Mary Wells;* **Only Love Can Break A Heart** *Gene Pitney;* **Palisades Park** *Freddy Cannon;* **Party Lights** *Claudine Clark;* **Patches** *Dickey Lee;* **Peppermint Twist** *Joey Dee & The Starliters;* **Ramblin' Rose** *Nat "King" Cole;* **Return To Sender** *Elvis Presley;* **Roses Are Red** *Bobby Vinton;* **Sealed With A Kiss** *Brian Hyland;* **She Cried** *Jay & The Americans;* **She Thinks I Still Care** *George Jones;* **She's Got You** *Patsy Cline;* **Sheila** *Tommy Roe;* **Sherry** *Frankie Valli & The 4 Seasons;* **Shout! Shout! (Knock Yourself Out)** *Ernie Maresca;* **Slow Twistin'** *Chubby Checker;* **Soldier Boy** *The Shirelles;* **The Stripper** *David Rose;* **Stubborn Kind Of Fellow** *Marvin Gaye;* **Surfin' Safari** *The Beach Boys;* **Twist And Shout** *The Isley Brothers;* **The Twist** *Chubby Checker;* **Twistin' The Night Away** *Sam Cooke;* **Up On The Roof** *The Drifters;* **The Wah Watusi** *The Orlons;* **Walk On By** *Leroy Van Dyke;* **The Wanderer** *Dion;* **What's Your Name** *Don And Juan;* **When I Fall In Love** *The Lettermen;* **Wolverton Mountain** *Claude King;* **You Don't Know Me** *Ray Charles;* **Young World** *Rick Nelson*

the beatles

Ringo Starr replaces Pete Best on drums.

Citing that "groups of guitars are on the way out," Decca Records rejects The Beatles after they audition for the label. The Beatles audition for producer George Martin at EMI-Parlophone in London, and he signs the group.

George Martin produces the single *Love Me Do* combined with *P.S. I Love You* at his first recording session with The Beatles and after 16 takes is satisfied.

The Beatles make their television debut, appearing on the BBC program *Teenager's Turn* to play Roy Orbison's *Dream Baby*.

Brian Epstein signs The Beatles to a management deal.

Peter Jones of the London *Daily Mirror* interviews The Beatles and concludes they are "a nothing group."

The Beatles are one of the opening acts for a Little Richard concert at New Brighton Tower, near Liverpool.

This is your first look
at the most exciting
eye-liner since eye-liner.

It's shiny!

Max Factor's flashing new, dashing new
Eye Liner stays shiny even
after it dries! It's waterproof
and dullproof. The specially
designed fine, fine brush is
all sable for the finest shine
ever. Get both right now
and see what a little Shiny
Eye-Liner can do...for your
eyes and for you.

New Shiny Eye-Liner
only by Max Factor

Record Of The Year
I Left My Heart In San Francisco
Tony Bennett

Song Of The Year
What Kind Of Fool Am I?
Leslie Bricusse &
Anthony Newley,
songwriters

Album Of The Year
The First Family
Vaughn Meader

Vocal Performance, Female
Ella Swings Brightly With Nelson
Ella Fitzgerald

Vocal Performance, Male
I Left My Heart In San Francisco
Tony Bennett

Rhythm & Blues Recording
I Can't Stop Loving You
Ray Charles

Rock & Roll Recording
Alley Cat
Bent Fabric

Folk Recording
If I Had A Hammer
Peter, Paul and Mary

New Artist
Robert Goulet

Awards presented in 1963 for 1962 music.

Literature

Pulitzer Prizes

FICTION
The Edge Of Sadness
Edwin O'Connor

HISTORY
*The Triumphant Empire:
Thunder-Clouds Gather In
The West 1763-1766*
Lawrence H. Gipson

POETRY
Poems
Alan Dugan

GENERAL
NON-FICTION
*The Making Of The
President, 1960*
Theodore H. White

PUBLIC SERVICE
**Panama City
News-Herald**

MUSIC
The Crucible
Robert Ward

Nobel Prize for Literature

John Steinbeck,
U.S.A.

"for his realistic and imaginative writings, combining as they do sympathetic humour and keen social perception"

President Kennedy *presents* **Robert Frost** *with the* CONGRESSIONAL MEDAL *in recognition of his contribution to U.S. literature.*

PASSINGS

Poet **e e cummings**, *whose penchant for lower-case letters and imaginative punctuation added to his uniqueness, dies at age 67.*

Mississippi native, Nobel and Pulitzer Prize winner, and former whisky runner **William Faulkner** *dies at age 64.*

1962 Advertisement

1962 Ninety-Eight Holiday Sports Sedan

Where style comes first...and quality counts!

For the discriminating buyer who demands "something extra"—it's the pace-setting 330-h.p. performance and trend-setting style of the magnificent

Ninety-Eight **OLDSMOBILE**

OLDSMOBILE DIVISION · GENERAL MOTORS CORPORATION

THERE'S SMOOTH POWERFUL V-8 ACTION IN EVERY OLDS → NINETY-EIGHT · SUPER 88 · DYNAMIC 88 · F-85 · STARFIRE

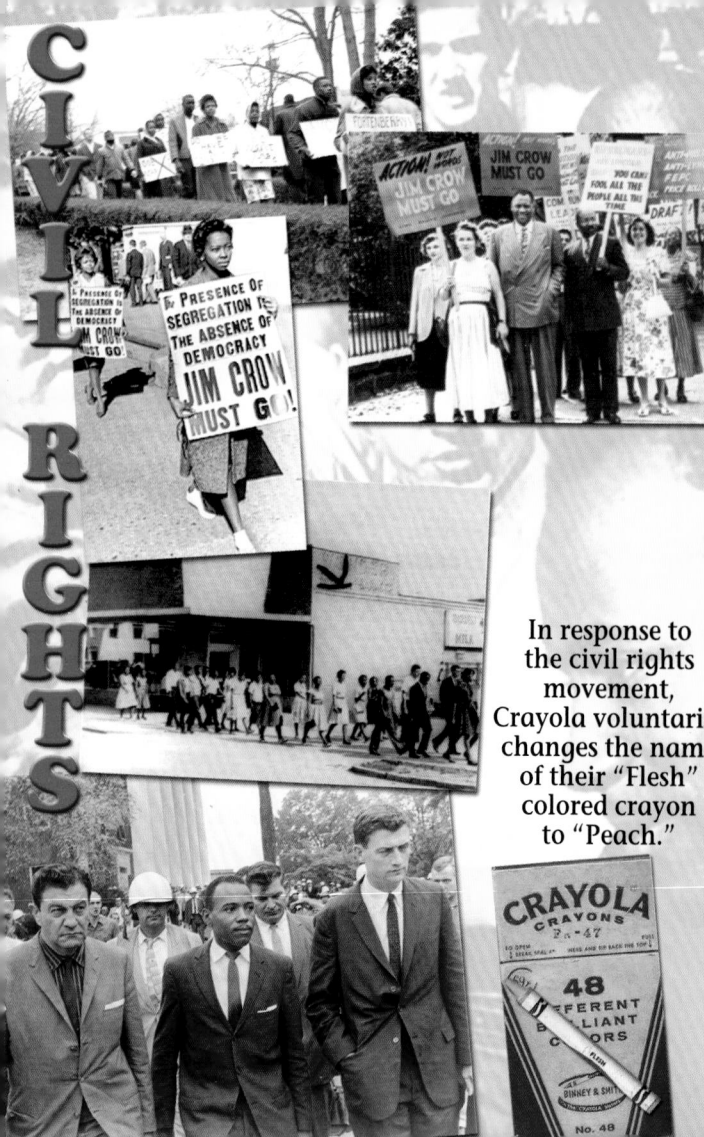

CIVIL RIGHTS

In response to the civil rights movement, Crayola voluntarily changes the name of their "Flesh" colored crayon to "Peach."

- Ordering the State of Mississippi to yield on integration, President Kennedy federalizes the Mississippi National Guard.

- The U.S. Justice Department files the first federal suit to end racial segregation in public schools.

- 33 public school districts are integrated this year for a total of 948 in 17 southern states and Washington, D.C.

- The U.S. Supreme Court reverses the convictions of six Freedom Riders.

- With the exception of the National Guard, the Defense Department orders the racial integration of all military reserve units.

- New Orleans' segregationists offer blacks free one-way bus tickets to northern cities.

- President Kennedy bars religious or racial discrimination in federally funded housing.

- Controversy surrounds James Meredith, an African American who wants to attend the University of Mississippi, when Mississippi Governor Ross Barnett tries to stop him from attending. Meredith is allowed to begin classes on October 1st, after a deal between Attorney General Robert Kennedy and Governor Barnett. Rioting breaks out and 200 people are arrested when Meredith attends classes.

- After defying orders to desegregate Catholic churches in New Orleans, three segregationists are excommunicated by Roman Catholic Archbishop Joseph Rummel.

- The worst race riot since 1910 breaks out on Thanksgiving Day at the District of Columbia Stadium during a high school championship football game.

this calls for

Budweiser®

the neighbors...out in the kitchen, swapping ideas with good friends. This is fun ...and this calls for Budweiser.

Where there's life...there's Bud.

News Around the World

MAKING HEADLINES IN 1962

A formal agreement is reached between the United States and Japan on the final settlement of U.S. postwar economic assistance to Japan.

After more than 300 years as a British possession, an agreement is signed to grant independence to Jamaica, making it an independent member of the British Commonwealth.

U-2 pilot Francis Gary Powers is freed by Russia in exchange for U.S.-held Soviet spy Rudolf Abel, sentenced in the U.S. in 1957.

The Irish Republican Army announces the end of its campaign of violence against the partition of Ireland. Great Britain releases political prisoners following IRA peace offer.

Canada collects a $1 billion loan from the United States and the United Kingdom to help halt its economic slide.

Monaco's unwillingness to alter its status as a tax haven results in France abrogating its 1951 convention with Monaco.

Argentina becomes the 14th Latin American country to break diplomatic ties with Cuba.

Argentine President Arturo Frondizi forms a coalition with the military barring Peronists. José Maria Guido is sworn in as president after Frondizi is deposed and arrested by the armed forces. The Argentine congress and all political parties are dissolved by Guido.

The Republic of Rwanda and Kingdom of Burundi are formed, winning their independence from Belgium.

U Thant is unanimously elected U.N. Secretary-General by the General Assembly.

By a vote of 56 to 42, the U.N. General Assembly votes against admission of Communist China.

Uganda becomes the 110th member of the U.N.

The U.N. General Assembly votes to ask United Nations members to impose economic sanctions on South Africa until it abandons racial segregation.

U.N. forces are dispatched to the Congo to restore order in Stanleyville.

Soviets announce they will arm and train Cuban military personnel.

Senate resolution serving notice that the U.S. will use military force if necessary against a Cuban threat to U.S. security is approved.

Kennedy informs the nation about the naval and air "quarantine" on shipments of offensive military supplies to Cuba.

Castro mobilizes as the U.S. orders interception of 25 Soviet vessels in defiance of Moscow threat.

Soviet Premier Khrushchev orders ships to avoid blockade and suggests summit.

Moscow offers to dismantle bases in Cuba if the U.S. disbands bases in Turkey.

The Soviets challenge the right of the U.S. to stop shipments of arms to Cuba and say the Kennedy administration is risking nuclear war.

The Council of the Organization of American States votes unanimously to authorize the use of armed force to prevent shipments of offensive weapons to Cuba.

Acting U.N. Secretary-General U Thant asks the U.S. to cease the Cuban blockade and asks Russia to stop sending missiles. The U.S. states the blockade will continue as long as there is a missile threat.

A U-2 reconnaissance plane is missing and presumed lost over Cuba.

Khrushchev agrees to dismantle Soviet installations in Cuba and arrange for a U.N. inspection team. In return he wants the U.S. to lift the blockade and join other OAS nations in a commitment against invasion of Cuba.

U Thant flies to Cuba to confer with Castro on the details for a U.N. inspection. The U.S. suspends its naval blockade and air surveillance during Thant's visit. Castro tells him that Cuba will not accept inspection of military installations unless the U.S. agrees to five conditions, one being evacuation of the U.S. naval base at Guantanamo Bay.

Castro rejects any form of international inspection in Cuba.

Kennedy announces that aerial photographs indicate Soviet missiles in Cuba are being dismantled. U.S. surveillance continues until a means of inspection can be arranged.

Khrushchev announces that all Soviet rockets have been removed from Cuba.

Kennedy lifts the Cuban naval blockade following assurances from Khrushchev that all Soviet bombers in Cuba will be removed within 30 days.

42 Soviet bombers are shipped out of Cuba and returned to the U.S.S.R.

While visiting Florida with his wife, Kennedy tells a Cuban invasion brigade that had been captured in the Bay of Pigs attack that "Cuba shall one day be free again."

CUBAN MISSILE CRISIS

In the most critical period in history since the end of World War II, world peace is threatened as **Fidel Castro** and the Russians turn Cuba into an island fortress. **U.S.** planes spot missile installations aimed at key points in the Western Hemisphere and bring back evidence of a weapons buildup that moves the Organization of American States and the Western Allies to back **President Kennedy** unanimously when he declares an arms blockade of Cuba and issues an ultimatum.

"To halt this defensive buildup, a strict quarantine on all offensive military equipment under shipment to Cuba is being initiated." Kennedy further announces, *"All ships of any kind bound to Cuba, from whatever nation or port, will, if found to contain cargoes of offensive weapons, be turned back."*

...LY **NEWS**
...York's Picture Newspapers 5¢

LOCKADE
A ARMS

...eds If Castro Attacks

Cuban Blockade;
If Castro Attacks

...es U.S.
...Aggression

The Washington Post **FINAL**

...edy Orders Blockade of Cuba
...eds Build Nuclear Bases There;
...Will Sink Defiant Arms Ships

1962 Advertisement

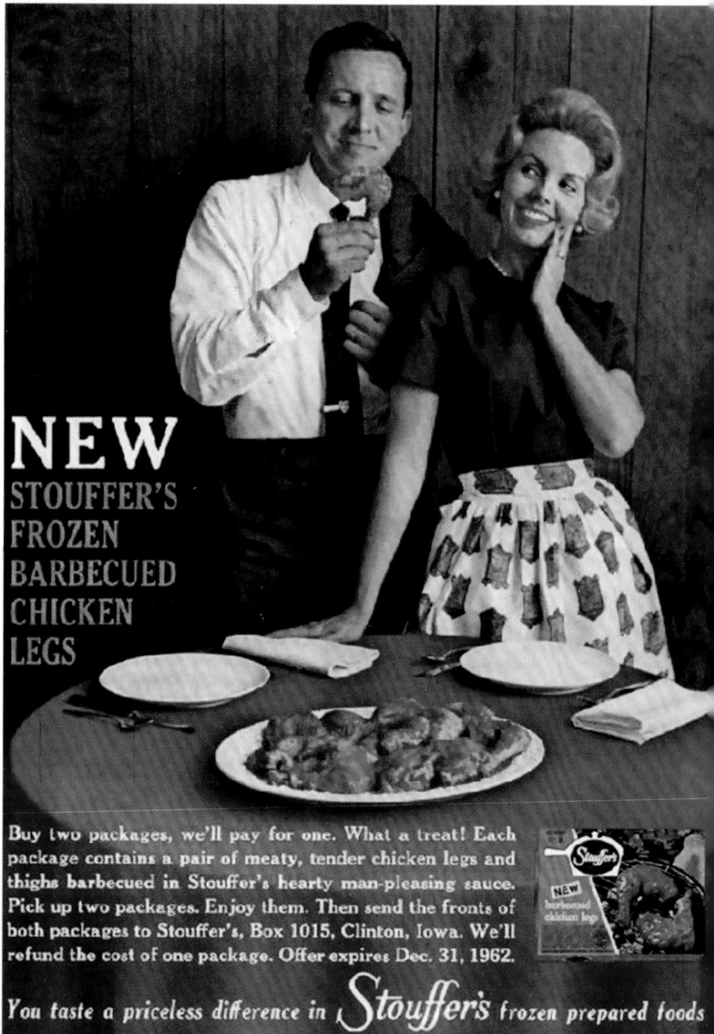

NEW
STOUFFER'S FROZEN BARBECUED CHICKEN LEGS

Buy two packages, we'll pay for one. What a treat! Each package contains a pair of meaty, tender chicken legs and thighs barbecued in Stouffer's hearty man-pleasing sauce. Pick up two packages. Enjoy them. Then send the fronts of both packages to Stouffer's, Box 1015, Clinton, Iowa. We'll refund the cost of one package. Offer expires Dec. 31, 1962.

You taste a priceless difference in *Stouffer's* frozen prepared foods

Massachusetts Democrat John W. McCormack is elected Speaker of the House at the second session of the 87th Congress of the U.S.

Young Americans for Freedom choose Republican Senator Barry Goldwater as their presidential candidate in the 1964 elections.

In the largest voter turnout in a non-election year, Democrat Edward Kennedy wins the Massachusetts Senate seat.

Richard Nixon launches his bid for governor of California by accusing Governor Edmund G. Brown of ignoring the threat of Communism.

Defeated California gubernatorial candidate Richard Nixon concedes, announcing, "You won't have Nixon to kick around anymore."

A U.S. constitutional amendment to bar the poll tax as a requirement for voting in federal elections receives congressional approval.

The U.S. State Department issues new regulations denying passports to members of the Communist Party.

President Kennedy requests authority from Congress to spend up to $2 billion on expanded public works programs if unemployment figures indicate a recession.

Kennedy asks U.S. Congress to authorize the tripling of the Peace Corps and signs a bill authorizing the Peace Corps to expand to approximately 10,000 volunteers.

In a special message to the U.S. Congress, Kennedy asks for $1 billion to expand federal recreational areas.

Kennedy calls for a consumer protection plan covering food, drugs, cosmetics and television sets. Kennedy signs the Food and Agriculture Act of 1962 providing for some increased crop controls.

Kennedy signs a bill permitting stricter federal control over employee pension and welfare plans.

Calling it unnecessary and undesirable, President Kennedy rejects immediate federal income tax cuts.

In an effort to destroy Viet Cong food supplies and to defoliate their hiding places in the jungle, "Operation Ranch Hand" begins, which calls for the spraying of pesticides along a 70-mile route leading to Saigon.

Two Americans are killed an ambush in Vietnam north of Saigon.

U.S. Defense Secretary Robert McNamara reveals that U.S. military training personnel in South Vietnam have returned the fire of Communist guerrilla forces.

Nam Tha, the royal government stronghold, is captured by Pathet Lao rebels in Laos.

Ships and over 1,000 Marines are dispatched to Laos by President Kennedy to counter Communist gains.

4,000 U.S. troops are sent to Thailand to aid Laos.

Public gatherings without police authorization are banned in South Vietnam.

Calling it a clear breach of the cease-fire in Laos, President Kennedy condemns attacks by pro-Communist troops.

Headed by Prince Suvanna Phuma, a new coalition Laotian government is installed.

The last U.S. Marines are withdrawn from Thailand.

Declaring the buildup of U.S. military in South Vietnam a threat to Communist China's security, The Chinese foreign ministry demands immediate withdrawal of all U.S. personnel.

The Soviets warn that war could result if U.S. military action against Communist guerrillas in South Vietnam continues

France is at peace for the first time since 1939. After seven years of bitter fighting between French and Algerian rebel forces, the war in Algeria comes to an end as 98% of French voters endorse the Algerian cease-fire in a referendum authorizing French President Charles de Gaulle to enforce the settlement.

Despite terrorist acts by the French Secret Army Organization, Algeria wins its freedom ending 132 years of outside rule.

Ahmed Ben Bella, organizer of the insurrection that led to independence, is elected premier of Algeria and soon finds himself beset with a score of problems. As the new nation faces economic collapse, Ben Bella turns to President de Gaulle for help.

Back in France, President de Gaulle calls for a national referendum on a constitutional amendment that would change the method of electing the president from the electoral college to direct popular vote.

In Paris, General Raoul Salan, former leader of the French Algerian Secret Army Organization, is sentenced to life in prison.

30 people are arrested in Paris in a plot to kill de Gaulle.

Hundreds of Europeans flee the violence in Algiers.

Algeria joins the United Nations.

Moscow accuses Israeli diplomats of using synagogues for espionage activities.

The first secretary of the U.S. Embassy in Moscow is expelled on spying charges, the second U.S. diplomat ordered out of the Soviet Union within seven days.

Following the removal of a U.S. tank near the East-West Berlin wall, the Soviets withdraw 12 tanks.

Great Britain, France and the U.S. lodge protests to the Soviets against the dangerous Soviet harassment of their flights into West Berlin.

The Soviet government lowers military draft age from 18 to 17.

Moscow says it will defend China against any invasion.

1962 Advertisement

Wollensak Stereophonic Tape Recorder
Model T 1515-4, under $250 at fine music
and photography stores everywhere

Wollensak means precision in sound! Just touch a button, sit back, relax. Let the magnificent Wollensak Stereophonic bathe you in sound, rich, and full-bodied as only stereo tape can bring it to you. Listen to the sound of the world's greatest voices, triumphal orchestras captured precisely by the exclusive Wollensak "Balanced-Tone." Know the unique pleasure and satisfaction of owning a Wollensak Stereophonic ... of playing 2 and 4 track stereo tapes, or recording and playing up to 8 hours single track. Dual speed, 10 watts of power. See it, hear it now.

Wollensak

AN AFFILIATE OF **3M**

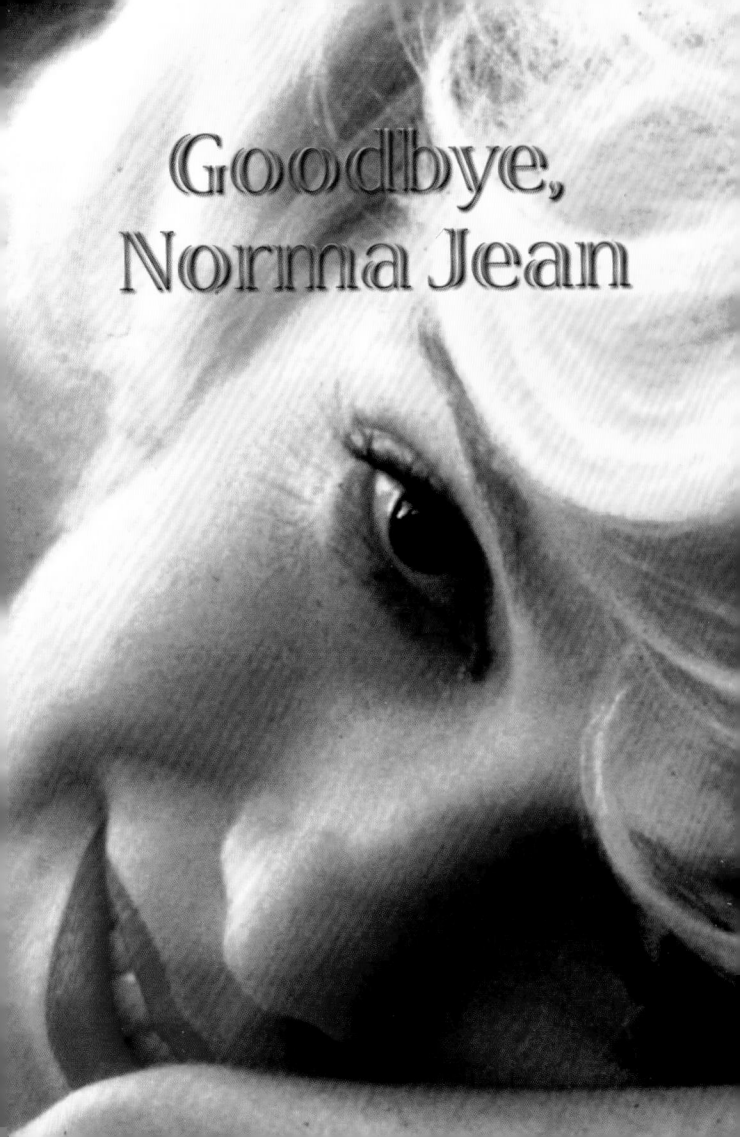

Goodbye,
Norma Jean

Marilyn Monroe Dies At Age 36

On August 5th one of the most famous stars in Hollywood history is found dead in bed under circumstances that are in tragic contrast to her glamorous career as a comic talent, for on the surface she seemed to have such a zest for life.

She found no happiness in marriage. Her second husband was baseball immortal Joe DiMaggio, and the marriage ended, as had her first, in divorce. Her third husband was playwright Arthur Miller and they too separated.

Monroe played in 23 films since her debut in 1950, films that grossed over $200 million. The "Golden Girl" received 5,000 fan letters a week. And to those fans, she never let any personal problems dim her screen glamour.

The star led a far from normal childhood and had 12 sets of foster parents, leaving her to say in her last interview that she was unaccustomed to being happy and it wasn't something she ever took for granted. Despite flashes of temper tantrums, she turned in performances that kept her among the greatest box office favorites in motion picture history.

Marilyn Monroe's will is filed for probate with more than half of her $500,000 estate going to "The Method" acting coach, Lee Strasberg.

At Marilyn Monroe's crypt, Joe DiMaggio makes arrangements to place fresh red roses there twice a week forever.

CRIME TIME

Ex-Tito aide Milovan Djilas is arrested in Belgrade for his book on Stalin.

Convicted Russian spy Robert A. Soblen flees to Tel Aviv, Israel to avoid going to prison for wartime espionage against the U.S. and commits suicide in London where he was awaiting deportation to America to serve his prison sentence.

The U.S. indicts Teamster Jimmy Hoffa for accepting $1 million illegally from a Detroit trucking line.

In Texas, Billie Sol Estes is found guilty of a real estate swindle.

A Texas court declares controversial land financier Billie Sol Estes bankrupt.

Walter Winchell does an impromptu interview with racketeer Frank Costello at New York's posh Stork Club during which Costello reveals that he's been married to the same girl for almost 40 years and that his $27,000 fine for income tax invasion is about the same amount of money he would bet on a horse. Stripped of his citizenship by a U.S. district judge in 1959, Costello loses his attempt to reverse the deportation order, which will send him back to his native Italy.

1962 Advertisement

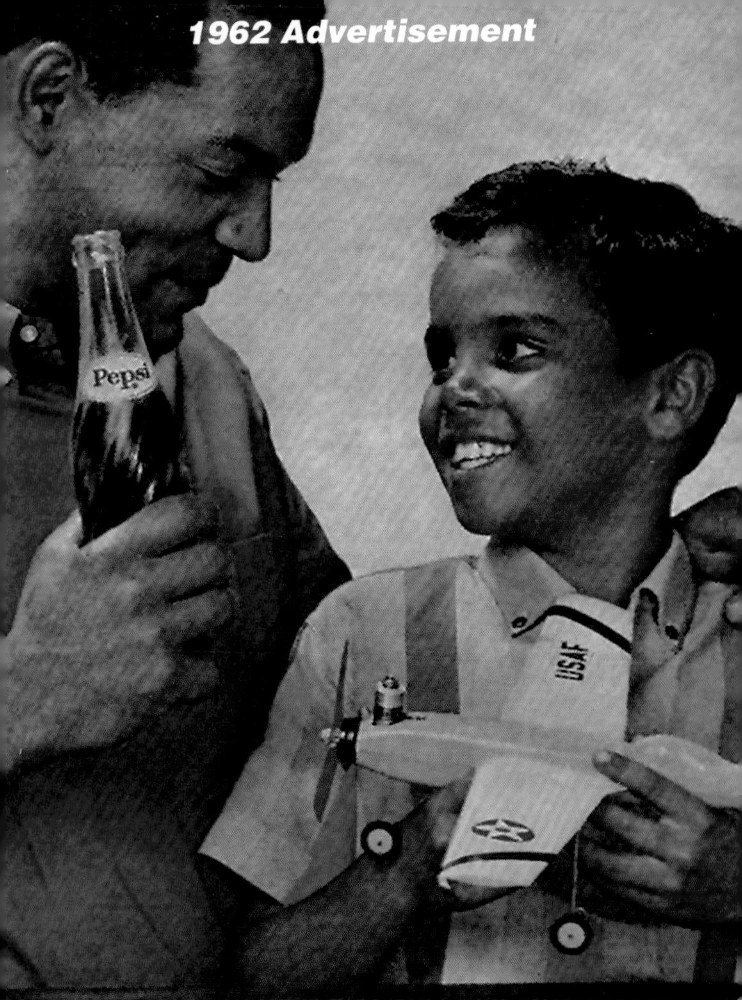

now it's Pepsi-for those who think young

Thinking young is a state of mind. Any age can join in. Today you see it everywhere —people are more active, doing more things. This is the life for Pepsi—light, bracing, clean-tasting Pepsi. Think young. Say "Pepsi, please!"

1962 Advertisement

Cans store compactly!

Cans chill fast!

No deposits! No returns!

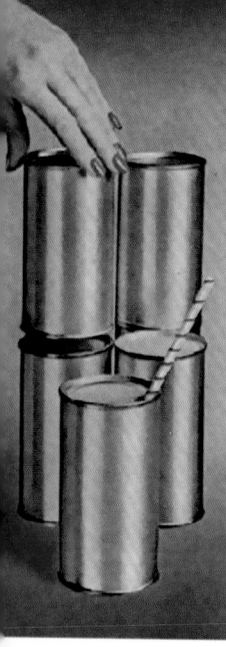

Live it up a little—with handy steel cans! Cans save space. Save time. Save work. Remember—no deposits, no returns when you buy soft drinks and beer in steel cans.

Steel

for Strength
... Economy
... Versatility

BETHLEHEM STEEL

BETHLEHEM STEEL

KENNEDY HAPPENINGS

President Kennedy receives honorary degree from Yale University.

JFK becomes the richest president in U.S. history when he receives another fourth of his share in three trusts established by his father, Joseph P. Kennedy, bringing JFK's share to $10 million.

The president purchases a 39-acre piece of property near Middleburg, VA and plans to build a ranch-style home on it.

The President and the First Lady visit Mexico City on their first trip to Mexico.

President Kennedy is mobbed by hundreds of swooning bathers as he takes a dip in the ocean in Santa Monica.

Jackie guides millions of television viewers on a tour of the White House in an hour-long program aired simultaneously by NBC, ABC and CBS.

In addition to Mexico, Jackie visits Rome, where she has an audience with Pope John XXIII; England, where she lunches with Queen Elizabeth II; Pakistan; and India.

In Groton, CT Jackie christens *Lafayette*, the world's largest submarine.

Attorney General Robert F. Kennedy goes on an informal goodwill tour of the world. 100,000 West Berliners welcome Bobby and his wife, Ethel, during a bitter cold snowstorm.

Edward Kennedy admits being thrown out of Harvard for cheating on exams.

In May, Marilyn Monroe dazzles a crowd of 15,000 gathered at Madison Square Garden to honor President Kennedy's 45th birthday when she sings "Happy birthday, dear Mr. President" swathed in a skintight, flesh-tone gown.

Celebrity Headlines

Actor **Mickey Rooney** files for bankruptcy in Los Angeles Federal Court.

Imitating the antics of **Elizabeth Taylor** and **Richard Burton**, **Mike Nichols** and model **Suzy Parker** in cahoots with photographer **Richard Avedon** stage a brawl in a Paris nightclub to garner publicity for gorgeous new Paris fashions.

17-year-old **Swoosie Kurtz**, daughter of pilot Frank Kurtz, who flew the second most famous bomber in World War II called the Swoose (A-bomber Enola Gay is #1), enters the University of Southern California to study drama.

Tom Brokaw graduates from the University of South Dakota and begins his career in journalism.

Elvis Presley gets a visit from Priscilla Beaulieu who flies from West Germany to visit him over Christmas.

Oxford University honors 73-year-old Englishman **Charlie Chaplin** with a Doctor of Letters degree for the pleasure he has given people over the years.

World War II beauty queen **Veronica Lake** is found working as a combination hostess, waitress and barmaid in the pub of a women's hotel in New York City.

Actress **Jayne Mansfield** and her husband, **Mickey Hargitay**, survive a harrowing night after being marooned on a small coral island six miles from Nassau in the Bahamas.

Milton Berle administers mouth-to-mouth resuscitation for 20 minutes to a man having a heart attack at Las Vegas' Sands Hotel and saves his life.

French sex kitten **Brigitte Bardot** awakes in a hotel room in Fiesole, Italy and discovers poet **Domenico Buono** kneeling at her bedside and reciting poetry, at which point she screams and has him arrested.

In Israel, **Frank Sinatra** is presented with a key to Nazareth and a silver-embossed Bible, and attends the groundbreaking ceremonies for the Frank Sinatra International Friendship Youth House.

Sinatra battles with 50 neighbors over his right to establish a private heliport outside his home in the Coldwater Canyon section of Beverly Hills.

Sinatra is terribly angry when on a visit to California **President Kennedy** opts to stay at **Bing Crosby**'s house in Palm Springs instead of the new "Presidential Wing" Frank built just for JFK and retaliates by eliminating the president's brother-in-law, **Peter Lawford**, from his luncheon list.

LOOKS LIGHT

Burgermeister has the lightness because it has the ingredients finer ingredients grown for lightness, selected for lightness and then brewed for lightness. So naturally Burgie looks light, tastes light, drinks light glass after glass after glass Try todays Burgie in the bright new package

TASTES LIGHT

DRINKS LIGHT

glass... after glass... after glass

Wedded Bliss?

[E]lizabeth Taylor and her husband, **[E]ddie Fisher**, adopt a one-year-old [o]rphan.

[F]isher, resting after spending a few [d]ays in a private psychiatric hospital [i]n Manhattan, denies there is anything going on between his wife and [h]er *Cleopatra* costar, **Richard Burton**. Fisher laughs off rumors of his [n]ervous breakdown and possible [b]reakup of his marriage. The "unro[m]antically involved" *Cleopatra* [s]creen couple are later seen in Rome [d]ancing and kissing.

[B]urton has a rendezvous with his wife, **[S]ybil**, in Paris where they picnic with [th]eir children.

[T]aylor is rushed to a hospital in Rome [w]ith a case of food poisoning and re[f]uses to see her husband, Eddie, who [f]lies in from Portugal to be at his [w]ife's side. He is allowed to escort her [h]ome the next day.

[E]lizabeth issues instructions to her at[t]orney to terminate the services of her [f]ourth husband, Eddie Fisher.

[E]lizabeth and Richard have a spat in [a] Rome nightclub.

[E]lizabeth and Richard arrive in Lon[d]on to begin filming *The V.I.P.s*.

Married in '62

Frankie Avalon
&
Kay Diebel

Jack Lemmon
&
Felicia Farr

Janet Leigh
&
Robert Brandt

Sean Connery
&
Diane Cilento

Rex Harrison
&
Rachel Roberts

Dick Clark
&
Loretta Martin

Zsa Zsa Gabor
&
Herbert Loeb Hutner

Jon Voight
&
Lauri Peters

Vanessa Redgrave
&
Tony Richardson

SCIENC

In conjunction with NASA, Bell Telephone Laboratories launches Telstar, a 170-pound satellite used to relay television programs from the U.S. to Europe and vice versa as well as other types of communication.

A New York newspaper sends 5,000 words to Paris at a rate 16 1/2 times faster than radio or cable using the Telstar communications satellite.

To help with their homework, engineering students at Case Institute of Technology are being supplied with experimental portable analog computers the size of six cigarette packs that can integrate, add, subtract and multiply.

U.S. and Russian scientists agree on world weather watch which calls for increasing the number of observation centers, collecting, analyzing and disseminating weather information and cooperation in launching weather satellites.

In a joint project between Britain and the U.S., the first international satellite is fired into orbit at Cape Canaveral.

Using echo sounding, the British Navy reports a record oceanic depth of 37,782 feet in the Mindanao trench east of the Philippines.

& MEDICINE

Norman F. Ramsey, Daniel Kleppner and H. Mark Goldenberg of Harvard University develop an atomic clock that will gain or lose only a few seconds in 100,000 years.

Nobel Prize winner Dr. Francis H.C. Crick of Cambridge University excites the scientific community with his experiments designed to crack the genetic code by suggesting that the four chemical bases of RNA always arrange themselves by threes. With a letter standing for each of the four bases, 64 three-letter "words" would be possible, with the trick being to find the 20 words that represent each of the 20 amino acids, the building blocks of protein.

Using a donor from outside the family, the first human kidney transplant is performed.

The severed arm of 12-year-old Everett Knowles, Jr. is successfully reattached after he loses it in a train accident.

The first use of a laser in eye surgery is used at New York's Columbia-Presbyterian Medical Center.

Dr. Russell H. Morgan, Director of Radiology at Johns Hopkins Hospital, develops a system whereby moving images of X-ray examinations can be recorded on magnetic tape via a television tape recorder which can be played back instantly, allowing the doctor to evaluate the patient.

Thousands of deformed babies are born in Europe as a result of mothers taking a sleeping aid called thalidomide. Dr. Frances O. Kelsey, of the U.S. Food and Drug Administration, averts similar American tragedies by preventing the drug from being sold in the U.S., for which she receives the President's Award for Distinguished Service from President Kennedy.

As a result of the thalidomide tragedy, Congress passes the Drug Amendments Act of 1962.

NOBEL PRIZES

CHEMISTRY
Max F. Perutz
(Great Britain)

John C. Kendrew
(Great Britain)

PHYSIOLOGY OR MEDICINE
Francis H.C. Crick
(Great Britain)

James D. Watson
(USA)

Maurice H.F. Wilkins
(Great Britain)

PHYSICS
Lev D. Landau
(USSR)

1962 Advertisement

HOWARD JOHNSON'S "LANDMARK FOR HUNGRY AMERICANS"
RESTAURANTS · MOTOR LODGES · 45 ROCKEFELLER PLAZA, N. Y. 20, N. Y.

Americans Orbit Earth

On February 20th *Friendship 7* blasts off into space with **John Glenn** at the controls. Glenn is the first American to orbit Earth, and upon completing three orbits he returns to Earth and is greeted with a hero's welcome. Next up is **Scott Carpenter**, onboard *Aurora 7* on May 24th, who successfully completes three orbits. The third American to orbit Earth is **Wally Schirra**, who completes six orbits onboard *Sigma 7* and returns safely to Earth on October 3rd.

President Kennedy and John Glenn inspect *Friendship 7* at Cape Canaveral.

The Soviets set another space first by sending twin manned spacecraft into nearly identical orbits with the first spacecraft *Vostok 3*, piloted by **Andrian Nikolayev**, orbiting Earth a record 64 times. *Vostok 4*, piloted by **Pavel Popovich**, follows two days later with the second pilot orbiting 48 times in 70 hours and 57 minutes.

Clockwise from left:
John Glenn,
Wally Schirra,
Scott Carpenter

A party in every pitcher! Only Kool-Aid brings you so much fun in such delicious flavors. One 5¢ package makes 2 quarts of pure, wholesom refreshment. Look for your favorite flavor in this bright new package

New Products and Inventions

Corning Glass Works invents a new process called Chemcor, which tempers glass chemically, making it up to five times stronger than any previously known glass.

Touting it as one of the most important new products the company ever developed, IBM introduces a computer designed for small and medium-size businesses with programs for payroll, sales and billing.

The Destroyit Super-Speed, a paper-shredder the size of a typewriter and capable of shredding up to 500 pounds of paper per hour, is available from Michael Lith Sales Corp. of Manhattan.

To protect your youngster in the car you can now put him in a new molded car seat with its own seat belt, locked into the car by using the car's safety belt.

An easy-to-install pocket paging system that operates on radio frequencies has been developed by Multitone Electronics, Ltd.

Using a built-in record player with replaceable records and batteries, a new doll called Chatterbox recites almost 50 words when you press her button.

Faster than dial phones and capable of transferring incoming calls to another number, the 10-button push-button phones go into commercial use.

Slumber Tone, a new device that emits a comforting sound thought to be the same as what the baby hears in the womb, is attached to the crib or carriage where it will lull your little darling to sleep.

RCA has developed a dictating device that will print your words on paper, provided you stick to its present 100-word vocabulary capability.

Completed in December 1961 at a cost of just $4.5 million, the iconic Seattle Space Needle is officially open to the public on the first day of the Seattle World's Fair, April 21st.

An experimental plant in the Los Angeles area sponsored by Lockheed Aircraft is turning garbage into marketable products.

Skin diver Sam Raymond of Watertown, Massachusetts has invented a waterproof plastic camera case making it possible to take pictures underwater with the Polaroid Land Camera.

The packaging industry is using a newly developed can with a "pull-top" for easy opening.

Chicago's Armour & Co. offers housewives instant bacon for the first time, which cooks in three minutes vs. nine to twelve minutes for regular bacon.

Sweetened with cyclamates, Royal Crown Cola puts out Diet Rite Cola, the first sugar-free cola.

The dandiest dads make Aunt Jemimas!

Hooray!
It's
Aunt
Jemima
Day!

GREAT SHAKES! SAUSAGE DOT PANCAKES! It's easy
Just shake up some Aunt Jemima Pancake Mix. (May w
suggest Buttermilk in the blue package.) Place slices o
cooked pork sausage links on griddle in clusters. Pour Aun
Jemima Pancake batter over clusters and bake to a golde
brown. Flip and brown other side. That's it! They're great

Apples (lb.)	$ .10
Avocados (each)	.10
Bread (loaf)	.21
Broccoli (lb.)	.10
Butter (lb.)	.69
Cabbage (lb.)	.05
Cheddar Cheese (lb.)	.64
Chocolate Malt	.20
Coffee (lb.)	.59
Cucumber (each)	.10
Donut	.07
Eggs (dozen)	.45
Fruit Pie	.39
Ice Cream (1/2 gallon)	.49
Lemons (lb.)	.10
Mayonnaise (qt.)	.49
Milk (gallon)	.28

HOUSING
3-Bedroom House
National Average	$11,800
Memphis, TN	8,675
Levittown, NY	13,390
Englewood, NJ	26,500
Malibu, CA	35,000
New Canaan, CT	39,900
Prefabricated House	3,599

Sam Walton opens the first Wal-Mart in Rogers, Arkansas.

• • •

The first Kmart store opens in Garden City, Michigan.

Peanuts (lb.)	$ .39
Pineapple (each)	.29
Rhubarb (lb.)	.19
Rice (lb.)	.21
Sugar (lb.)	.11
Tomatoes (lb.)	.19
Women's Blouse	8.95
Women's Dress	25.00
Women's Gloves	4.98
Lipstick	1.50
Permanent	15.00
Men's Dinner Jacket	42.50
Men's Haircut	3.75
Necktie	2.19
Men's Polo Shirt	7.95
Men's Slacks	24.50
Men's Suit	85.00

YEARLY SALARIES
Bookkeeper	$ 6,500
Controller	15,000
Copywriter	7,800
Draftsman	8,000
Editor	8,200
Electrical Engineer	12,000
Executive Secretary	7,000
Home Economist	8,000
Insurance Claim Adjuster	5,200
Market Analyst	10,000
Military Personnel	3,800
Radio Program Director	12,000
Sales Analyst	7,500
Teacher	5,300

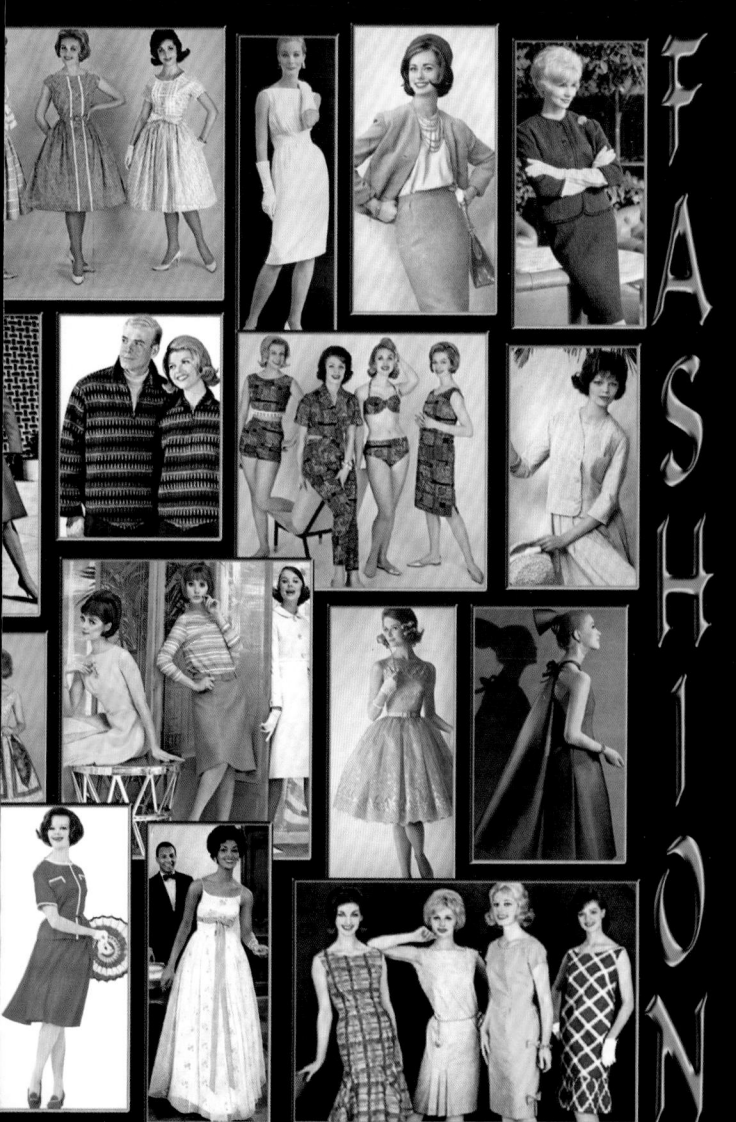

FASHION

1962 Advertisement

look what
Champale
tastes like!

the malt liquor you serve like champagne

It tastes like a celebration. It sparkles like a party. It tingles ... it bubbles with excitement. It goes with a big dinner ... with small talk ... with hors d'oeuvres or TV. It's so elegant, you'll want to serve it in your finest stemware. And one bottle fills four average champagne glasses—deliciously! Remember, where there's you and Champale—there's a party. Have some tonight

FREE! For clever new drink recipes, including the fabulous Champale Cocktail, write Dept. P, P.O. Box 2230, Trenton, New Jersey

... *costs little more than beer*

Champale

Metropolis Brewery of N.J., Inc., Trenton

BASEBALL

WORLD SERIES

New York Yankees over **San Francisco Giants** 4-3

HOME RUN LEADERS

_NL_ - **Willie Mays**
(San Francisco, 49)

_AL_ - **Harmon Killebrew**
(Minnesota, 48)

CY YOUNG AWARD

Don Drysdale
(Los Angeles)

MVP

_NL_ - **Maury Wills**
(Los Angeles)

_AL_ - **Mickey Mantle**
(New York)

ROOKIE OF THE YEAR

_NL_ - **Ken Hubbs**
(Chicago)

_AL_ - **Tom Tresh**
(New York)

BATTING CHAMPIONS

_NL_ - **Tommy Davis**
(Los Angeles, .346)

_AL_ - **Pete Runnels**
(Boston, .326)

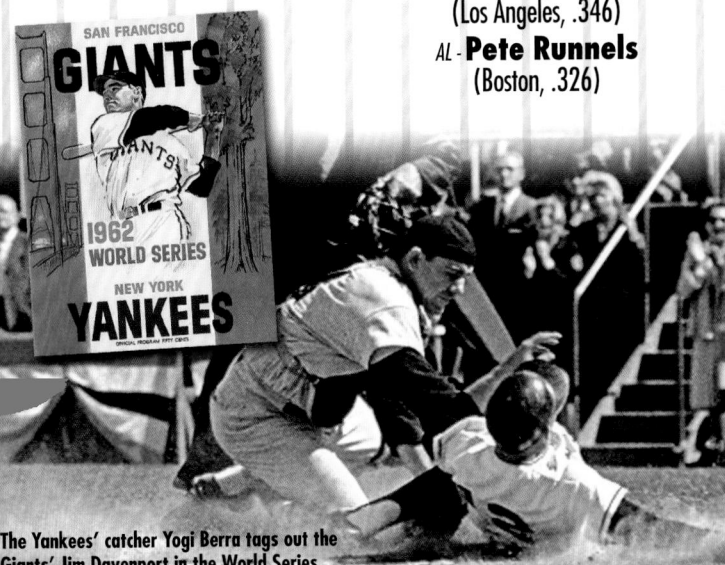

The Yankees' catcher Yogi Berra tags out the Giants' Jim Davenport in the World Series.

FOOTBALL

NATIONAL FOOTBALL LEAGUE CHAMPIONS

Green Bay Packers over **New York Giants** 16-7

AMERICAN FOOTBALL LEAGUE CHAMPIONS

Dallas Texans over **Houston Oilers** 20-17

NATIONAL COLLEGE FOOTBALL CHAMPIONS

USC

11-0-0

ROSE BOWL

USC Trojans over **Wisconsin Badgers** 42-37

ORANGE BOWL

Alabama Crimson Tide over **Oklahoma Sooners** 17-0

SUGAR BOWL

Mississippi Rebels over **Arkansas Razorbacks** 17-13

COTTON BOWL

LSU Tigers over **Texas Longhorns** 13-0

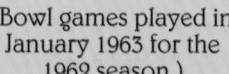

(Bowl games played in January 1963 for the 1962 season.)

I dreamed I took the bull by the horns... in my *maidenform bra*

1962 Advertisement

the face is America...

the 'special sparkle' is Canada Dry

■ It's 'special sparkle' that makes Canada Dry Ginger Ale and Canada Dry true-fruit Grapefruit brighter, bubblier, and better tasting by far. Just the right amount of Canada Dry's famous pinpoint carbonation plus a blend of the finest, purest ingredients . . . that's 'special sparkle'. Sparkles you longer, sparkles you best! Are you planning fun in the sun? Have some!

A 'special sparkle' beverage for every taste

BASKETBALL

CHAMPIONS
Boston Celtics over
L.A. Lakers 4-3

MVP
Bill Russell
Boston Celtics

ROOKIE OF THE YEAR
Walt Bellamy
Chicago Packers

POINTS
Wilt Chamberlain
Philadelphia 76ers 4,029

REBOUNDS
Wilt Chamberlain
Philadelphia 76ers 2,052

NCAA CHAMPIONS
Cincinnati over
Ohio State 71–59

COLLEGE MOP
Paul Hogue
Cincinnati

In a game against the New York Knicks, Philadelphia 76er Wilt Chamberlain becomes the first player ever to score 100 points in a single game. The game is played in Hershey, Pennsylvania, and the fans go wild, forcing the referees to call the game with 46 seconds left on the clock.

BOXING

HEAVYWEIGHT
Floyd Patterson
Sonny Liston

LIGHT HEAVYWEIGHT
Archie Moore
Harold Johnson

MIDDLEWEIGHT
Terry Downes
Paul Pender

WELTERWEIGHT
Benny "Kid" Paret
Emile Griffith

LIGHTWEIGHT
Joe Brown
Carlos Ortiz

FEATHERWEIGHT
Davey Moore

Emile Griffith regains the welterweight title he lost last year to **Benny "Kid" Paret** after beating Paret into a state of insensibility. Paret never regains consciousness and dies 10 days after the fight.

In what is billed as the "fight of the decade," **Sonny Liston** knocks out **Floyd Patterson** in two minutes and six seconds of the first round and walks off with the world heavyweight title.

Sonny Liston

Floyd Patterson

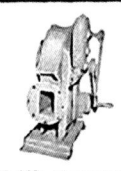
HOCKEY

STANLEY CUP CHAMPIONS
TORONTO MAPLE LEAFS
over
CHICAGO BLACKHAWKS
4-2

ART ROSS TROPHY
BOBBY HULL, Chicago

VEZINA TROPHY
JACQUES PLANTE, Montreal

CALDER MEMORIAL TROPHY
BOBBY ROUSSEAU, Montreal

LADY BYNG MEMORIAL TROPHY
DAVE KEON, Toronto

HART MEMORIAL TROPHY
JACQUES PLANTE, Montreal

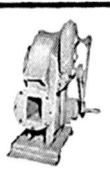
HOCKEY

STANLEY CUP CHAMPIONS
TORONTO MAPLE LEAFS
over
CHICAGO BLACKHAWKS
4-2

ART ROSS TROPHY
BOBBY HULL, Chicago

VEZINA TROPHY
JACQUES PLANTE, Montreal

CALDER MEMORIAL TROPHY
BOBBY ROUSSEAU, Montreal

LADY BYNG MEMORIAL TROPHY
DAVE KEON, Toronto

HART MEMORIAL TROPHY
JACQUES PLANTE, Montreal

1962 SPORTS HIGHLIGHTS

AUTO RACING

Indianapolis 500:
Rodger Ward

Le Mans:
Oliver Gendebien &
Phil Hill

FIGURE SKATING

U.S. Champions:
Monty Hoyt &
Barbara Roles
Pursley

World Champions:
Donald Jackson
(Canada) & Sjoukje
Dijkstra (Holland)

HORSE RACING

Kentucky Derby:
Decidedly ridden by
Bill Hartack

Preakness:
Greek Money ridden
by John Rotz

Belmont Stakes:
Jaipur ridden by
Willie Shoemaker

CYCLING

Tour de France:
Jacques Anquetil
(France)

Giro d'Italia:
Franco Balmamion
(Italy)

**World Cycling
Championship:**
Jean Stablinski
(France)

TENNIS

U.S. Open:
M - Rod Laver
W - Margaret Smith

Wimbledon:
M - Rod Laver
W - Karen Hantze
Susman

Davis Cup:
Australia over
Mexico

Australia's Rod
Laver becomes the
second man in
history to win the
grand slam of
amateur tennis.

CHESS

**World Chess
Champion:**
Mikhail Botvinnik
U.S.S.R.

U.S. Champion:
Larry Evans &
Bobby Fischer

GOLF

U.S. Open:
M - Jack Nicklaus
W - Murle McKenzie
Lindstrom

PGA/LPGA:
M - Gary Player
W - Judy Kimball

Masters:
Arnold Palmer

British Open:
Arnold Palmer

BOWLING

**BPAA All-Star
Tournament:**
M - Dick Weber
W - Shirley Garms

**ABC Masters
Tournament:**
Billy Golembiewski